UNDARK

AN ORATORIO

U N D

 a blewointment book

AN ORATORIO

ARK

NIGHTWOOD EDITIONS

2012

SANDY POOL

Nightwood Editions
P.O. Box 1779
Gibsons, BC von 1vo
Canada
www.nightwoodeditions.com

Nightwood Editions acknowledges financial support from the Government of
Canada through the Canada Book Fund and the Canada Council for the Arts,
and from the Province of British Columbia through the British Columbia Arts
Council and the Book Publisher's Tax Credit.

This book has been produced on 100% post-consumer recycled, ancient-forest-
free paper, processed chlorine-free and printed with vegetable-based dyes.

TYPESETTING: Carleton Wilson
COVER DESIGN: Blair Prentice

Printed and bound in Canada

LIBRARY AND ARCHIVES CANADA CATALOGUING IN PUBLICATION

Pool, Sandy
Undark : an oratorio / Sandy Pool.

Poems.
ISBN 978-0-88971-273-7

I. Title.

PS8631.O622U54 2012   C811'.6   C2012-903579-3

They make a noise like wings. Like leaves. Like sand. Like leaves. Silence. They all speak at once. Each one to itself. Silence. Rather they whisper. They rustle. They murmur. They rustle. Silence. What do they say? They talk about their lives. To have lived is not enough for them. They have to talk about it. To be dead is not enough for them. It is not sufficient. Silence. They make a noise like feathers. Like leaves. Like ashes. Like leaves.

—Samuel Beckett, *Waiting for Godot*

IN THE EARLY 1900S, thousands of women between the ages of eleven and forty-five were employed painting glow-in-the-dark watch dials for soldiers and civilians in both Canada and the United States. Under the guidance of the paint's inventor, Sabin Von Sochocky, they kept their brush points sharp by "pointing" the tips of the brushes with their lips.

Several years after leaving the plant, these women developed a variety of mysterious medical conditions, including complete necrosis of the jaw, severe anemia, intense arthritic-like pains, and spontaneous bone fractures in the arms and legs. A few of the former workers became lame when their legs began to shorten. When the women visited doctors, some were told it was syphilis that was causing their symptoms. Sabin Von Sochocky was forced to remove his own thumb due to necrosis, and eventually died of radiation-induced anemia.

Though many women tried to sue the company, the lawsuits were largely unsuccessful. Many of the women died before receiving compensation. The final demise of the US radium dial-painting industry did not come until Canadian production was halted in 1954, and the extraction plants in Belgium shut down in 1960.

Dramatis Personae
(in order of appearance)

Sappho: (612–570 B.C.?) Ancient Greek poet, born on the island of Lesbos. Included in the list of nine lyric poets deemed by the scholars of Hellenistic Alexandria as worthy of critical study.

Nox: a striking dark-featured woman in her late sixties, reminiscent of Marie Curie.

Radium Women: a group of factory workers ranging in age from eleven to forty-five years old.

Undark: a propaganda radio personality.

Chorus: a sea of light (voice-over).

Sabin: (1882–1928) scientist, and inventor of Undark radium-based paint.

Hatshepsut: (1508–1458 B.C.) foremost of noble ladies, fifth pharaoh of the eighteenth dynasty of Ancient Egypt.

(I) UNDARK

                              down wings

they let their

      [

      [

                              grew cold

Nox, Lucerne: 1905

Black. The thick of.
Men weave through

cobblestone streets, steering
wooly dark. Everyone knows

the watch painters, their overcoats
shimmering, speckled to

the waist. From here, uniforms appear,
reappear: glow-worms summoned to glide

and writhe through the sombre
square. If children wake

they peer through shutters,
incandescent hoods of the men's

hair. Soon enough, sun
blazes through alleys, dissolves

the luminous mass. But for now,
we watch. Absorbed, as if by music—

as if these men are treble clefs. Crooning
through pitch and timbre.

We make a noise: wings or ghosts
of bats. Two licks, two ticks. Or—

something beating something. At
night it enters. Our brush keeps time,

pressing onto. Out of. Two licks. Two
ticks. The beauty of bold strokes

pounding us still. Two ticks. Two.

Later we'll laugh, shake moonlight
off our clothes, like ash.

For now, a clock. The day
wears—worn mechanism.

Tick lick tick lick tick lick. We hear
the buzzer. Look to our watch.

Come. Meet us at the edge of the rail yard. Past
the European honeybee, the brook trout,

the ghost of Annie's road. Here, we lick
our lips, point brush tips, paint

dials in dayglow shades. On breaks, we ink
copperplate names on barrel drums,

dream a handsome soldier will hear
our licking hearts, read our handwriting

in the demi-lit pander. The tick
of it seesawing them to sleep.

We paint because our hands are delicate.
We paint because everything defines itself

in the end, because we're sick of leaning
away from light, ghostly

and tiring. At night, the teeth of our
hands aglow. Light only

the edge of what's
swallowed, consumed.

In the distance, our babies sleep
through the night. We sing lullabies

our mothers sang to us, sing them
aloud with nostalgia or fear,

as if we were waiting for the air to clear.
Our voices, still vibrant, and the sky so—

the railway, loud this time of year. Come, listen
to our pandemonium. Meet us at the edge of noise.

For if she flees

[
[
[

gifts

            she does not

[
[
[
[

soon, unwilling

                    Come heartlong [   ]

[
[
[

                    be ally

                                    00:36:18:693

Undark doesn't get dark in the dark. You want
Undark because it contains real radium and keeps its glow
for years. If the house number on your door glows in the dark with
Undark, people can tell it's the number they want without lighting
matches or ringing your bell to inquire. Soon we will paint your
rooms in moonlight. Luminous piano keys, conductor's batons.
We are miners and refiners of radium-bearing ore.
Pioneer manufacturers, largest in the world.
Soon you will demand Undark on everything.
Soon you will say: *I want that on mine.*

Nox, Newark: 1919

Flash light
pull chain

push button
door bell

safe lock
gas gauge

fish lure
toy eye

bed slipper
poison bottle

clock hand
door lock

flash light
pull chain

push button
door bell

safe dial
gas gauge

fish lure
doll eye

bed slipper
pill bottle

clock arm
door knob

old tooth
small box.

alone I lie. The hour goes by: middle night and Pleiades.

Moon set

[
[

1916

Next time you fumble for a switch, bark
your shins on furniture, wonder vainly what time it is
because of the dark—remember Undark.
Today, thanks to constant laboratory work
everyone can benefit from this
most unusual element. Twenty-three
years ago, radium was unknown. Today,
it serves you safely and surely. You must
ask yourself this: what would you like
to see in the dark? Fishing lures? Clocks?
Buckles on bedroom slippers?! Most assuredly you do.
Undark takes care of the dark, so you don't have to.
You may ask plainly: does Undark contain real radium?
Of course it does.

Salt of the earth, lie still. Wind, not enough. Salt. Bury it in the backyard, half-angry kiss. Corpse of this house, an assemblage we meant to say lightly. Say something, anything. Light takes so long to get to us. Here is the ash and ice, the frame, and the ice. An eye, stupefied. I thought all men were beautiful. Please, don't tell me.

desire delight took
[
[
[
all but
[
[
at once nor

to become
[

a yes [   ] Radiant lyre
[
[

[   ] speak

Sabin (i)

I dip wrists to
elbow; seize the mercurial

obsession of moths. My face
eats radium, becomes blooms

becomes stars, becomes birds, all
wings beating at once. Time,

I could hardly name her.
A twinge, a twinge. Uncanny

glow, like feathers, like leaves.
Safe as the love of test tubes

cradled in my palm. It is
radium, returned to me

like a lover—
yellow, all prospect. To state

this fascination, the hue
of indulgence, idolatry.

I return home late. My wife,
asleep. I run my neon hand down

the long line of leg. To touch
is to believe this—

ambitious as cells but something
else. Not guilt that flows

like ink but milk-blood: a monument
on the mouth.

The lab, deserted now, and quiet. The walls
shimmering aftermath.

Remember things beautiful

daring the opposite

[
[

                    these things we did and many things

in our youth we live [   ]for yes

                yes will you

Wind scars hillside awake. One night
in a million when we know we're in

love. It doesn't repel them. We come, dead-tired
to bed, slip into place. We've painted our teeth again,

and we laugh until he kisses us, tells us
there are other places we could paint, nuzzles

himself in. Outside, the groaning
suburbs, hollow yowl. Uninhabited

as any New Jersey night. Winded
as windows, howling at the moon;

we don't care. Our fingers trace
maps of stalled time, liquid silk

into skin. The factory empty now,
quiet. When he says we are glowing

he means it. On nights like this, even the shutters creak
sonata, all the necks of streetlamps bow like swans.

Small disappointments. Mason jars boiled, empty. Firelight burns for no one. If your eyes are blue, so be it. A small animal, perhaps a hare. I know. I know it already. Everything stops. Your skin, each empty door tells me.

delicate covered her woven up well

                    with cloths and

            [
            [
            [
            [
            [
            [
            [
            [
            [
            [
            [

1912

With the coming of electric light, it seemed, the last
step in illumination had been taken. But, already,
there is a supplement. No longer are electric
lights, the light of lamps, or candles necessary
to see things in the dark. Undark shows
them to you. Manufacturers recognize
the value of Undark. They have been painting
it on everything. No longer is it necessary to grope
aimlessly for a switch; the switch itself shines.

Sabin (ii)

The time will doubtless come
where you will have in your own home
a room lit entirely by radium. The light thrown off;
the colour and tone of soft moonlight.

—Sabin Von Sochocky

These paintings illuminate themselves;
resplendent teeth, gone nearly dim.

In a dark hallway, a woman
takes her medicine. She turns

to the mirror, passes out. Here is her
body, elegantly tired. Stomach

full of flashlights. There's something
I've been meaning to tell you about time:

isn't much. Still,
you say, you will have

everything. Atom active dust,
emanations. Nothing a quick gin

can't cure. In the dark you went on.
Six hours, seven. Thirteen

blood transfusions. Enough.
Here is a crucifix glowing

on a wall. Here is fish hook,
lure. Here is a toast to all the gals

you've loved before. Here
is a switch:

a room entirely lit. Pluto found tangled
in the dust of ruptured stars.

What can I say about bones? Sugared
honeycomb; the evening, unremarkable.

A glass of water, just a glass. It may be
useless now to say. Aplastic anemia.

My apologies dream of
a room in the light of a room,

a room lit entirely by

the light thrown off—

some man more

[
[
[

have forgotten me [   ] Or than me

                         [
                         [

                    of sleep black and on [   ] the eyes

Cold-hearted. The moon left you:
over-stuffed hug, thin metaphor.

Everything continues. The zucchinis
grow on. I drive past the cemetery listening

to Millocker. Well. Then. This poem
is about the time you spent waiting

for a series of distinctions.
Then. Yes. It. Is. It will take

three thousand years to void
the colour and tone of soft moonlight.

Say, then, shipwrecked and dishevelled: what do we know? This is our sweat, our exact weight, untold warmth, undisturbed bed. Line after line. Tomorrow I will go walking in the park, decidedly, the pinpricked night. Angry as dead photographs. All we ever see of stars.

00:26:13:376

[
[
[

For not become they

[

[

[

No, *not the moon but a clock dial gleams*
For me—and am I to blame
If pale stars look milky to me?

I hate Batyushkov's arrogance:
'What's the time?' they asked him once
And he answered, 'Eternity.'

—Osip Mandelstam

(II) HALF-LIGHT

1458 B.C.

 The light falters all

[
[
[
[

broken tooth
small box

Hatshesput

[   ] surprise

[
[

I know
what Knentkaues
knows

[   ] about scandal

Can you find the keyhole? Sometimes, even sober people
can't. If you have tried, at night, to locate a house,
you will breathe fervent blessings on radium, which shines
in the darkness like a good deed in a naughty world.
As for the keyhole, prohibition hasn't banished the problem
of finding it with neatness and dispatch. Radium has.
If only we could apply this method to political candidates!
But even the power of radium must stop somewhere.

It won't take long, that whimper:
noise that will not sing itself to sleep.

The waiting room proves we're in trouble. Haven't
been to the doctor's, been avoiding it. No

tolerance for bad news, intuition.
Ah well. There are always groceries,

the floor that will not clean itself. Or
something, or something else.

In the end, it isn't the sickness—
angry catacombs of sugar bone

miming calcium. No.
It's those damn descriptors:

Necrosis. Necrosis. Necrosis.
Why won't the man shut up?

1917

Success has brought imitators! Here, the purpose
of this advertisement—having made up your
mind to get an Ingersoll, you will actually
get it. Radiolites—genuine Radiolites (note
the name!) are made only by this company. No
other watch dials are Ingersoll. No other watch dials
are Radiolites. Another thing—outsiders are painting
in luminous shades. They are not Radiolites,
or Ingersolls. Do not forget the advantage:
a substance containing real radium. Please—
do not accept imitations! This advertisement is for
Radiolite. This advertisement is for your protection.

Thursday goes on confessing: moans, soft shoulder. Not one animal, but two. Anything. Say anything. Don't say it. Hardly enough to bury six years, night sky structure of certainty. What follows the night is what precedes it. Please, bury me by the turnpike. Please repeat the question.

1458 B.C.

At last you have seen
flesh

[

difficult iconography I know

[
[
[

you are looking
granite sphinx clawing
false beard

[   ] My body

Two obelisks blurring

But I

[
[

                              tell you arm broken
                              across heart cartouche

bearing name

Night like any April night. Cold
streetlamp, no relief. Lemon crocus

still poking through dirt, crown of her
stubborn head. From the window

the suburb is rapacious. Square
grids. We sit on the sill, peering

at tomcats buried under cars,
furtive and hungry.

The doctor told us we were
dying, or wouldn't deny it.

Either way, it seems strange to slip so
easily, slip so unexceptionally into sleep

and not wake up to make
breakfast or plait our hair.

It's easy to give up on
maple keys, sun firing down.

In the end we do what love tells us—
we get up again and again and again

until we can't. And
some nights are like that.

black of dream

[

roaming you

          [   ] hold terribly from pain

[
[
[
[
[
[
[
[
[
[
[
[
[
[
[
[

but not but may it happen.

In the dark we went on;
six hours, seven.

Nothing could stop us. The trees bristled
and shook. Outside the day circled

geese circled, blaring at nothing.
Handkerchiefs spoiled—

glowing linen in the dark. We are
jellyfish iridescent. Six hours

our face, white negative. Seven.
Our breath burns.

Let us put it this way:
luminescence, but no name.

1458 B.C.

contempt [   ]

Flank   .

[   ]   dug up

breasts   obscured

desecrated

[   ] Please
stop

Sabin (iii)

to make time
as if it was steadiness;

hospital corners, closets
begging for air.

Slight wheeze, white-washed. The
white-cloaked men come, talking

of who knows what. Tulips,
once pin-straight, flopped over in an orange

plastic cup. And I know it, I already remember:
remember buying fruit, or walking

the dog, or listening to Brahms. I remember
dancing with a lampshade on,

licking lime pulp from the side of
glass on a sticky morning, eating

ice cream off a giant metal spoon. These machines
did not occur to me: they whir-suck

their beeping, sterile measurements, but I
am not. There.

When I wake, in the white starch of
hospital sheets, I turn to you, say:

I held a pine-green praying mantis in my hand;
it was so squirmy, I just couldn't bear loving it.

We lapse into being the pond, frozen over. Hand cut with a dull knife, unsteady footsteps against your frame. The moon, silent kitchen. To demand these repetitions. Please, stop. Geese moving in the wrong direction, winter icing over trees. I know about white—sickening bone.

We swaddle babies tightly to our breasts,
feed them diligently. The anemia so bad—

bones pulse from pits like water wells;
we stare into them, looking for nothing.

Isn't enough, dull tenderness. Our babies
grow weak from songs. Everything

we give them. We telephone our mothers,
static soughing the end of the line.

What should we say? The newspapers rename us:
painter-girls, legion of the doomed,

we don't care. On Saturdays, we take
our babies to the water-tower hill, cherry

red toboggans in tow. It seems
the doctors have forgotten

these frozen afternoons—
how they last.

Nox, Newark: 1928

Of course there were inspections—
corsets glowing to the waist, the

discharge of a runny nose, candescent.
The women told quietly to stop

licking, keep radium out of their hair. At night
the factory was a constellation. Gemini—

a gleaming hourglass. Workbenches
brilliant as celestial maps. The legion

of the doomed waiting to die, waiting
on a court date. Outside, the sky

darkened a little, shadows
changed.

1921

Ever bruise your anatomy in the dark? Knock over
the bric-a-brac while hunting for the chain
on the table lamp? Paw the air for various artifacts?
Thanks to radium, night is being robbed of sundry terrors,
of knocking over the telephone and electric lamp, or rudely
encountering the corner of the bed while straining
on all fours for those elusive bed slippers! One of these
beacons will keep you off the rocks of rocking chairs
in midnight cruises about your sleeping room.
Friendly as lighthouses, they chart your course.
Of course, luminous gun sights are also made
for hunting in dark woods, late in the day;
and if you have ever held a shotgun
to your shoulder to bring down birds
you know what I mean.

1458 B.C.

Who is left to pull me from myself

[
[
[
[
[
[
[
[
[

To undo and undo this mandible would be to speak. Osseous tissue; we're sorry. We have nothing to say (we meant to say softly) the slightest articulation, marrow, temporal bones. We're sorry, we have to say. Line after line, our sickness. Forgive us.

Who says we want to live in this
world anyways? Ruinous lexicons pounding

our ears. This, we know:
dim rooms, bodies

bright as slogans. Fingers pressing
onto, out of. It's simple. We paint

because the 'money's good. Because
we serve our soldiers any way

we can. We arrive home after
the nightshift, eyes eaten

by intimate details. How we
illuminate everything—

perfect brushstrokes, a lover
sweeping hair from our eyes.

Please, stop. Your silhouette. Cut it out. Scapula. Accusatory trees. Stop. No leaves rosy-cheeked, glittering teeth, so be it. Here is my hand. Enough. Once I loved everything, patron saint of inconveniences; light moving across the table, dull-eyed, feverish pitch. Dear one: I've said nothing.

Nox, New Jersey: 1998

Beyond the range of the human ear
the cemetery clicks into being.

The earth groans. Each one to herself.
Silence. Rather, they whisper.

Skeletal lace, the larynx.
Worms undoubtedly disturbed

by the echolocation. Women
are speaking. To have lived

is not enough. They have to
reverberate like elbows

poking through undergrowth.
The rate of pulses rising

to terminal buzz. Women
like whale music, singing

under the newly mowed lawn:
lick tick lick tick lick tick.

To be dead is not enough.
The Doppler shift of history

buries them deeper. Geiger
counter clicks into being.

1458 B.C.

myrrh scarabs

[

Damnatio memoriae

                              no plebian eye
                              upon permanent

[
[
[
[
[
[
[
[
[
[
[
[
[

Sabin (iv)

Here I am. Empty courtyard, eyelashes
frozen. How long it takes—

my hands lose feeling, swell up. I stay
into the evening, shivering

in shirt sleeves. *Sabin—*
Go home. But I won't. Courtyard

crumbles beneath me. There is nothing
to be said of windowsills, of irony.

I stand in the snow for hours, pocketed
test tube, small heartache. Wish

I was still in Vienna, drinking coffee
from a thick glass mug, staring vacantly

out a bay window. One by one, the
women speak to me like swan-maidens.

To be dead is not enough; they need
to talk about it. Valkyries

at work, the healthy ones titter
behind my back. I know what they say—

*Crazy Sochocky who hacked off his thumb,
cried that he didn't love anyone.*

If only I had the strength to reach
them, to touch them with my wounds,

like the word that became flesh
and lived among them.

I'm not adherent, but I remember
that hymn: *Let all mortal flesh keep silence*

*and with fear and trembling stand. At his feet
the six-winged seraphs, cherubim*

with sleepless eye. Please,
let them know me by my scars.

It must all be this:
meagre cicada

chirping the dark—
this noise. Not enough

to drown the nubile
tick, the terrifying

pressing inward.

Our hands rustle like
foliage, our throats

tremble.

Sabin (v)

Stare at the wall. Unsightly mechanics
of clock, of bureau. To be completely

silent, or slip entirely into elongated
night. But that is only part of it:

room considers this existence, order
of doors and bedrooms, shadows

efflorescing on a wooden floor.
These stars are women, points

of brightness. They sleep in my bed
tousling the sheets, the light

thrown off. Room considers
how the world does not end—

ticks out in mediocre time, empty
as air. I am in my death-room

that no one will visit. The ghost
of my thumb, still throbbing.

The death, no. I am not afraid of—
but the dark, the noise. I have

already given what I can afford,
sin-sacrifice.

Please, bury me in the ruined
lyric cemetery.

companions

[
[
[
[

these things

[
[

shall sing

beautiful

00:09:50:429

It will not love you. To discuss these repetitions. Safe solace, our quarantine: to be so good, so terrible. It will not love you to discuss these repetitions. Please: stop.

Sabin (vi)

You and I meet on such a night
at the city limits;

when I say it, my mouth bleeds
an illicit alphabet, sounded

on terrible ancient teeth.
I'm sorry, I have nothing. You

women are waiting to become what you already
are, what you already have been.

There is an archive of this
emptiness. You meet it again

and again, meet it in the loneliness of
sick beds, in the lengthening

light. You meet it with snarls of blood
leaking from your mouths.

You meet it solemnly,
because you know nothing

ends until you want it to, nothing ends
in waiting rooms or hospitals, or all-

night coffee shops. The light simply
dissipates, disappears.

You women are driving me mad
with your eyes pointing at everything.

I'm sorry I have nothing to say,
please repeat the question.

someone will remember us

[

I say

[

another time, even.

00:08:04:003

1458 B.C.

Please say nothing

[

soon dead

                           Moses floats

Nile crowned in salt

        [   ] face rots

Bright bone shine nail-less
fingertips

        [
        [
        [
        [
        [
        [

In the courtroom we sagged
in rows. Too sick

to take the oath, judge
eyed us insects, black

mantis hearts, ticking.
Ah well. There are always

lawyers, their summer vacations.
To imagine things differently:

July filled with strawberries,
straw hats, drinks with straws

in them. Instead, our spines
telescoping, feet dead

sparrow curl, crippling
sarcoma. The judge consults

his calendar, adjourns.
Objections, overruled. We'll

meet him again in September—
with our inky compound eye.

Sabin (vii)

The history of radium is beautiful.

—Marie Curie

Here, glimpse. Truths
that ruin you: angry signatures,

lawyers on summer vacation.
I'm sorry. There will be no

settlement. No solace for
your bones. You are too

weak to raise your hands,
to take the oath. You are

too weak to speak of irony.
Now all of you will die, hair

saturated with the sparkling dust
of summer. They will accuse you

of venereal disease, force words
into mouths, like wounds:

black ink, the brush-off. I'm sorry.
There is nothing to say. Even

the dentist won't treat you.
Jawbones hollowed—ravaged

by honeycomb moths. Your throats
wax light: thick, ancient.

This is the story. It starts, as it
does, with romance

which mutates into mystery. It
doesn't matter what happens,

how it ends. You already know
the ending. Somewhere

in the suburbs, your husband
stands in the front yard, body stiff

with injury. From this angle, the dying
sun almost touches his face.

This is the story I meant to tell you:
pile of leaves burning ruby

in the background, how everything
flickers, then goes out.

When the trial finally resumes, three
of us are dead. Haunted by open hands,

words carried in mouths for hundreds of years.
To hear

morning hit the white clapboard fence—
cantering, mottled hope. To feel quiet

polished by an evening's peace
precisely because we cannot have it, because

when we first hear birdsong, we wonder
what it is. We feel thirst, salt-lustre

of tongues—customary sequence. Hours,
decades. Even the bleat of cars doesn't wake us—

our eyes turn opal. Please, bury us
where the sound starts. Bury us by the angry

scowl of the turnpike. Detritus clangs this
sound that isn't sound.

It fills our bellies
with seconds, with dust.

1458 B.C.

This is the essence

[
[
[
[
[

blood royal

I too had forgotten

[

someone

[

will remember another
time even

I have told you that the story of radium
is an unfinished story, and this is what I meant.
We used to believe, and doubtless you were taught, that
an atom of matter is indestructible. We do not believe
this anymore. Suppose we could make atoms of radium
obedient to our will. We would get, as a result, a tremendous
explosive power. As I have said, one gram of radium
could raise the Woolworth Building one hundred
feet in the air. Huzzah! To hope that we shall learn to control
radium is optimistic, but it is not a wild dream. You have
read the story of the stars. You know that the universe is
so vast. The man who tries to understand becomes
humble, because he knows very little indeed. The result
would be far greater than you imagine. Unless,
of course, you have an excellent imagination
and a considerable knowledge of chemistry.

Nox, Toronto: 2011

Each answer began with a lie:
hospital bedpans, tight corners.

Dead factory on Davenport. Lick
tick of it. Sleep—

no. Let me have this cool, this
street corner, this newborn.

Everywhere I look; ghostly
furniture. Paperwork. Paint

dry bone. This repetition left
us wanting. Here a

picture, complete thought.
It was still possible then

to imagine one or two hands
moving to face the hour.

But now we remember little
or nothing. The art deco

window traps flies in
sinews of screen. Paint

chipping off the sill
as the cold comes up.

In the winter, I cooked kale. Small arguments, emptiness of snow. Nothing happens, not yet. No bone to pick. Offer this small song. Stop, please: let it sing. Your hand as safe as last year. Here is a casement of longing. I've looked at you, seen hands, hoarfrost like eyelashes. No. A circulatory system.

Please, say nothing. There is never enough. Snow, bitter. Unable white against darkening.

00:00:26:567

Nox, Epilogue

Since then, I've hated
the dark. I never turn off the lights.

Notes and Acknowledgements

This book contains textual elements from a variety of early advertisements for Undark paint and other radium-based products. It also includes excerpts from reports written by Sabin Von Sochocky addressing the public about radium, and found text from Anne Carson's *Fragments of Sappho*. This book is also highly indebted to the work of Russian philosopher and literary critic Mikhail Bakhtin, specifically his excellent essay "Forms of Time and of the Chronotope in the Novel."

The writing of this book was made possible by the Ontario Arts Council, the Toronto Arts Foundation, the Banff Centre, the English Department at the University of Calgary, the Killam Trusts, and Diaspora Dialogues.

For their editorial assistance during the writing of this book I would like to thank John Barton, Baron Jeramy Dodds, Carolyn Forché, Robert Majzels, Jan Zwicky, and the Creative Writing Workshop at the University of Calgary. I would also like to thank Dr. Ross Mullner and Claudia Clark for their excellent research and advice on the Radium Dial-Worker tragedy, and a big shout out to Nikki Mills, Sachiko Murakami and Blair Prentice for all their mad skills.

I am also indebted to the following peers, teachers and friends who are the wickedest of the wicked:

Thom Pearson, Dozie Onuora, Dog Sandy, Shelagh Rowan-Legg, Leah Esau and the Esau family, Laura Lush, Brandon Ramako, Jen Balen, Jessi Cruickshank, Lindsey Clark, Sarah Flanagan Jacqueline Briggs, Mike Rocha and Fionnuala, Sheniz Janmohamed,

Jake Mooney, Jeff Latosik, Dave Brock, Erin Thompson, Dave Miller, Lexi Von Konigslow, Hollie Adams, Carly Stewart, Rod Moody-Corbett, Jon Flieger, Erina Harris, Derek Beaulieu, Ryan Fitzpatrick, Christian Bök, Jim Ellis, Claire Lacey, Kathleen Brown, Heather Osborne, Susan Toy, Sarah Ivany, Robyn Read, Jake Kennedy, Kevin Macpherson Eckhoff, Rebekah Dawn, Kelly Drukker, Sam Cheuk, Brendan Mcleod, Leah Kotsilidis, Sarah Mian, Susan Steudel, Greg Koop and family, Maurice Mireau, Virgil Grandfield, Alisa Gordaneer and family, Christina Kozak, Brooke Stubbings, Jordan Tannahill, everyone at the Banff 2012 writing studio, and the University of Guelph and University of Calgary Creative Writing programs.

Very special thanks to Silas White, Lizette Fischer, Marisa Alps, everyone at Nightwood Editions, Daniel Sadavoy, my family, and especially baby Jocelyn: this book is for you.

a blewointment book

IN 1963, BILL BISSETT founded blewointmentpress in Vancouver and began publishing mimeographed magazines of experimental poetry. Within a few years bissett, known for his own work in sound and concrete poetry, began to publish books that subversively extended the boundaries of language, visual image and political statement, including work by bpNichol, Steve McCaffery, Andrew Suknaski, Lionel Kearns, Maxine Gadd, d.a. levy & bissett himself. Meeting wide acclaim and controversy, the activities of blewointmentpress have had a seminal influence on the Canadian literary community.

After a drastic reduction in government support in 1982, the press stuggled with debt and bissett sold blewointment. It was renamed Nightwood Editions by Maureen Cochrane & David Lee. After a couple more incarnations of the press moving bissett-like back and forth across the country and publishing work as diverse as poetry, fiction, film & music criticism and children's titles, Nightwood launched a "blewointment" imprint in 2005 to honour bissett and the press's innovative, political and visual roots.